Awakening
My Sleeping

oetess

by

Sandra Ann Humphreys

PUBLISH
AMERICA

PublishAmerica
Baltimore

ISBN: 978-1-4489-9258-4
PUBLISHED BY PUBLISHAMERICA, LLLP
www.publishamerica.com
Baltimore

Printed in the United States of America

MOTHER'S SWEET WHISPER

Solitude is her pain
I cannot easily endure
But I love her so much
And instantly as I care
What can I do?
I am not a miracle worker
But I pray for a miracle
Please heal her Lord...
And my life is meshed with hers
My flesh and blood
For I am lonely too, and out of the game
Because I am not so strong
At least not as strong as her
I am too sensitive sometimes
And I just pray she can rely on me
For I am not always there
When I want to be
I hear my shame, I feel my guilt
Trying not to be bitter about the past
Angry and frightened
But in a sweet whisper
She calls to me

MY MOTHER

She carried me
And so I was born
I am still young
But oldness craves her
My lost thoughts
She regains
And leads me on
For we learned yesterday
And we will do tomorrow
Right now we live
I love her always
In dearest regards
Try to forget the rage
And not be so angry
I pray that I will follow God's path
And live in a world of surprise and wonderment

MOM

Her delight is a specialty rare
On a crimson light dinner she'd prepare

Her soft-spoken wisdom is to appreciate
No longer so many miles to separate

She can heal a body broken
With the tender words that she has spoken

And lift a spirit from low to high
She can relax your mind so that you can sigh

God gave to me a part of her
The love I need helps to endure

He gives me blessings from up above
In the form of Mother and her sweet love

I hope that Mom feels better soon
And knows I think she hung the moon

With all God's love that's understood
I think of Mom and my thoughts are good

WHILE SHE SLEEPS

While she sleeps
Her dreamy eyes full of thought of the night
Pain runs its course every day

While she sleeps
I dream that today God shows mercy
To all of us and makes her pains go away

While she sleeps
Echoes of time pursue her body
In cold retreat and follow through

While she sleeps I cry too
I live it out as she might suffer
And I feel so blue

She can smile
She can cry and she can run
But she can't hide
While she sleeps

March 15, 2004
To: MOM
Love from: SANDY

When your mind is full of worry
And the light in your eyes is pain
Just remember how sorry I am
I've hurt you once again

With my eyes set in the mirror
I see myself in vain
For without my need to love you
I will never love again

So, if you still feel startled
Because my bark is much worse than my bite
Remember that God loves you
And he'll keep your heart alright

When you'd rather I was absent
Because of tears I might make you cry
I'll always need your understanding & forgiveness &
unconditional love
As time on earth goes by

HURTOLOGY

Remains the death of my lost relationship
Sets of stories you told
Casts of clowns acting out
Degrading the experience of the end
The soft unspoken
Words
Secrets of your devilish repute
You lied and manipulated me
Stored up against the inadequacies I felt
To teach my heart the horrid things about you

CONGRATULATIONS

There's nothing so exciting
As a new baby so helpless, so playful, and so tiny
His first word was mommy or daddy who knows
Forget all that...now he's walking and look at how he goes...
"Now do as you're told!" that's the first rule
Especially today cause it's your first day at school
He's got his diploma and everyone is so proud
And so is his girlfriend, she's cheering in the crowd
Just today they got married it happened oh so fast
Being just a little boy is so far back in the past
She's nine months and nervous just waiting for a sign
The hospital is so crowded they have to wait in line
His mom and dad are here now their eyes lit up with joy
They walk towards their baby
Saying "Congratulations son!" it's a baby boy!!!

AN UMBRELLA BUILT FOR TWO

Under an umbrella built for two
Two lovers can be true
Sharing an umbrella built for me and you
As the rain falls down upon us
We're connected
No longer rejected
Holding hands
Under an umbrella built for two
Even under stormy skies
A cloud cries
But we're delighted, our songs all righted
Under an umbrella built for two

A TURN-AROUND

It's a turn-around
Your love turned upside down
It's a turn-around
Your love for me

It was a waiting game
No two days felt the same
My love put yours to shame
Right from the start

It's a turn-around
Your love turned upside-down
It's a turn-around
Your love for me

I'm glad the games will end
And you'll be my best friend
We won't need to pretend
That's what you'll be

No more for loneliness
It's true love I confess
No more hearts in a mess
Dreams will come true

It's a turn-around
Your love turned-upside down
It's a turn-around
Your love for me

I'LL LOVE YOU JUST THE SAME

My heart beats wild in rhythm
Just mentioning your name
I can get along just fine
I'm no ones latest flame
Sometimes I can't keep up with you
But I love you just the same

I'd love a dozen roses, some flowers by that name
You may forget, but you can bet, that I'll love you
just the same
I'd love a diamond ring my friend, a promise by that
name
It would shine so brightly, and I'd love you just the
same

Loneliness is with me now
As the night beings to fall
I wish someone were with me now
Cause I need them most of all
I can see the light ahead
But it's hard to play the game
I hope someone will come to me
And they'll love me just the same

I'd love a dozen roses, some flowers by that name
You may forget, but you can bet, that I'll love you
just the same

I'd love a diamond ring my friend, a promise by that name
It would shine so brightly, and I'd love you just the same

THERE IS THE LORD

There is the Lord in heaven above I call my lifetime friend
He's been the help in times of need, and Lord until the end

With wisdom not forsaking me, He shows me truth and light
The only thing I have to do, is confess in prayer tonight

Telling God I have done wrong, I ask help to repent
He knows if I am willing go change, then strength is heaven sent

Forgiveness, he has granted me, for I believed he died
So when temptation comes my way, humility conquers pride

I pray, dear God, when guidance need, I find you in my heart
And forever, with your guiding light, we'll never be apart

Consider this my friend, you see, in humble praise I seek
To be close to God, in peace, & love, and grow to stay as meek

I've finally grasped what my temptations are, and I find I'm free
to choose
To turn from sin, and walk away, and win, (with Christ) by choice
to lose

There is the Lord in heaven above, I call my lifetime friend
He's been the help in time of need, and Lord until the end

INSTRUCTIONS

Please read my love instructions
Handle me with care
I won't retreat to loneliness
When it's my Saviour that I share

I just cannot operate
The way I'm supposed to
If I don't read God's manual
Because I won't know what to do

Strangers don't have my love instructions
Neither parents, nor family
But Jesus has a plan for me
And it will set me free

Please read God's instructions
They are written on my heart
And If I separate from God
He'll teach a brand new start

Lord let me draw nearer to you
As I'm thankful that you're there
When I've turned from love instructions
And it's hard for me to care

Once more I find the Bible
With the instructions that one needs
To put their life back together again
After Satan's evil deeds

WALKING ON THE CEILING

We'd say "HI, Dad!" when he came home, we'd no longer
wear a frown
We were walking on the ceiling, when he turned us upside
down

I'd fall asleep on the couch, on purpose, but I guess Mom
knew
So that when he got home, he'd pick me up and tuck me in
too

Mom said he was my "Shining Knight" and I had to admit it
was true
I loved both my Mom and Dad, the short time I had available
to

When my Mom and Dad broke up, our family was totally
shattered
All that was left was chronic sorrow, and pain was all that
mattered

"Pick out any coat you want, and I'll buy your favourite
shoes!"
But when Dad left our home and went to hers, I was mixed
up and confused

Memories of the boat and island fishing, and teaching us to
swim
It seemed God's plan was perfect, so we left it up to him

The burgers on the "Coleman stove" and Mom's potato salad
I thought this song of Heaven, was sung just like a ballad

Our family trips to Florida, "Mickey Mouse" and ocean shells
*Slushies at 7-Eleven on a really hot day, just like a fairy tale
tells*

*Mom and Dad used their best life skills, and the information
that they had*
*A jealous man tried to hurt us, but God knew that he was
bad*

*I'll remember all the Christmases, the "Light Bright" and
"Lucky Locket Kiddle"*
*New skates and "Easy Bake Oven," but we were pawns
trapped in the middle*

*Now my parents are passed away, but they taught don't just
trust what you feeling*
*But to trust God to know right from wrong, and walking on
the ceiling*

LONG AGO

I don't really know what happened so long ago
But parts of it I remember
A stolen kiss from a bottle of bliss,
when you said that you're mine
It happened so long ago where did you go?
The pain was a promise broken
the unkind sweet words spoken
You really took me for a ride,
but the Northern lights were out of sights
I didn't want to worry so I went along
but my dreams were shattered everywhere
The day I found out and about
you never were really mine never really a friend at all
It was my young love forever true
but it was your abusiveness
I was a child
I hurt deep
So hope to feel so much joy when I heal

EXPLOITED

Exploited by adult things too young
I'm only seven, not twenty-one
Exploited by adult things too young
I'm only twelve not thirty-one
Exploited by adult things too young
I'm only fifteen not fourty-one
Exploited by adults isn't fair
I'm only sixteen, and you don't care
Being exploited you tried to ruin my mind
My mental health's a mess because you were unkind
I was too young to decide to have sex, do drugs or alcohol
Bi-Polar, Schizoaffective, MPD, and Post Traumatic is now what I'm called
Exploited by adults things too young
Only God's love can undo the damage done

THANK YOU, LORD

Thanks to you Lord, I'm a best friend
And thanks to you, I can have one too

The summer heat, makes our remarks
The hurtful words, that break our hearts

Even though our towns, are several miles apart
We can still be friends, and hug each other's heart

Please Lord continue staying, by each other's side
Spring, summer, winter, and fall, and always be our guide

Let what stands between us, never tear us apart
And if it ever tries to, may we make a brand new start

I'm not jealous Lord, for your love is true
I am healing faster now, and know better what to do

So I say thanks to God, I can be a best friend
And I can also have one, on earth until the end

TEARDROPS

Little teardrops in my eyes, rivers of pain
I may go insane
But you may make the sky go blue
By being you

Where's my spirit goin
While lifer is showin
Me
Sometimes it's not so clear
Lord draw me near

Little teardrops in my eyes
Rivers of pain
I may go insane
I may go insane
But you can make the sky go blue
By being you

I'm lost today, please show the way
I'm lonely but I can count on you
To lift the blue
But I still need the quiet
Why don't ya try it

Little teardrops in my eyes
Rivers of pain
I may go insane
I may go insane

IN MY HUSBAND'S ARMS

I long to be embraced under a starry, summer night
In his arms
My heart has just erased
My weary that's not right
Here in his arms...

I dream of loving you...do you see it in my eyes?
Can you hear it in my voice?
When our names become two sighs...

Is their hope in your expression?
Is their fate from your direction?

Can you see it in my eyes?
When the moon lights up the skies?
From a starry, summer night
In your arms
My heart has just erased,
My weary that's not right
Here in his arms...
Dear Lord, where is my husband to be?

I'd feel fine in the skin I'm in
If we were loving, skin to skin...
My heart has just erased my
My weary that's not right...In his arms...

GOOD-BYE MAN

He's a good-bye man
Leaves you hanging on
He won't be there tomorrow
He'll be on the run

He loves you for a little while
And even he'd confess
That once he was there for you
Just as long as you'd say yes

He just isn't someone
To stay with very long
He just has no interest
In singing your love song

I bet that he'll grow weary
Of telling all the lies
He's only after just one thing
As he's done so many times

He's the one your mother
Should've warned you all about
And just because she didn't
You'll cry & scream & shout

THE STANLEY CUP

For instance if the game is lost

In the player's playoff race

Those who were on the team that lost

Must still do so with grace

When the athletes place their blades on ice

To win hockey's greatest prize

The road could be a rocky one

And still take many tries

When all psyched up to win the game

They must play their very best

As each play-off series does begin

They must play better than the rest

The score, the timer, check the mark

The puck as aimed achieved

For trusting in the pass that's played

The goal is first believed

All of hockey respects the cup

Lord Stanley gives to winners

Because each player has embraced the thought

Since they were just beginners

FOLLOWING TODAY

You may follow me
I may follow you
Our steps together
May be forever true

        Eyes that follow
        Dreams that sigh
        I wish that I could hold you
        As the days go by

It would mean so much more to me
If we shared our love
And a gift from the heart
Is a gift from up above

        Eyes that follow
        Dreams that sigh
        I wish that I could hold you
        As the years go by

        I felt so sad to see you go
        Meaning you're not the one
        I pray the time away from love
        Will next time seeds be sown

I see your photograph
And I wonder what you thought
When somebody took it
It makes me smile a lot

Eyes that follow
Dreams that sigh
I wish that I could hold you
As the time goes by

A COFFEE AND A KISS

Except for you, a coffee, and a kiss
There's nothing that I really miss
My heart just rests its beating
Cause angels take love that's not repeating
I always thought you were the one
Cause my whole life's became undone
Except for you, a coffee, and a kiss
There's nothing that I really miss
St. Valentine is surely grieving
Our promise of love not yet believing
Except for you, a coffee, and a kiss
There's nothing that I really miss
But I'm glad I knew a friendship like this
You're so special, a coffee, and a kiss

TROUBLE

Trouble is evident now
Pushing through somehow
What we believe tomorrow is the risk at hand
Because today we take a stand
All is settled for now
The cast must take a bow
Also today, I cannot say which entrance
Or which exit seems to be the right way
On the edge of time I see
Which is my reality?
Where are you Lord?
And suddenly I feel you near...
Please be granted that through my faith you are

SUZI

Suzi shines like a diamond
Precious and rare
She lifts me up
And takes me everywhere

So much like an angel
So much like a child
Grown up but indifferent
And just a little wild

A friend of mine
I help her see
The things I know
That help to set her free

Just like a rainbow
In a summer sky
It seems only natural
That we're naturally high

Now we're best friends
And will always be
At least until
We're at least ninety three

CRAZY EYES

You blinked at me with those crazy eyes, a good disguise
You entered into the tiny place, with a smile upon your face,
But you were no stranger to me
And your magic lit up the space

Your crazy eyes were fixed on me
A look I can't forget
Something told me we'd met before
It seemed a certain bet

I miss the look, with those crazy eyes
But I had to turn away
Then I looked back into your eyes, feeling no surprise
And then went along my way

It was so nice when you spoke to me
A man of great dimensions
I hope I get to see you again
And greet your good intentions

Goodness here I go again
Feeling lost but holding true
I won't forget to count to ten
Then get over missing you

"AT 27"

When you're one year old impressed are most
One year it's been since greeting your host
When you are ten two digits make your age
It's Mickey Mouse to baseball that now becomes the rage
At thirteen you're called a teeny-bopper
By your over-the-hill brother who insists that it's quite proper
When you reach the sixteenth year
You're sweet and noticed and sneak a beer
Eighteen is, or so it seems, the year we dream more adult dreams
At twenty-one you're legal world-wide
And it becomes quite common on a mate that you'll decide
Twenty-five is when you're told, that you are now a quarter century old
Thirty-year olds sometimes fit the bill
Of old folks who are over the hill
At fourty you know life begins
And strangers ask for forgiveness of sins
At sixty-five years of age
We close a chapter, not the book
At this stage

But at 27 who knows what you're up to...

THE WALLS

The walls of painted pictures
And taped on photographs
Can hardly soothe my memories
Of pain, or gain, or laughs

The walls I seem to focus on
And blink once more to see
Remind me that I'm by myself
But I don't want to be

The walls that now protect me
From heat & cold extreme
Keep me inside from the rain
And cause my heart to dream

The walls that now surround me
Create this tiny room
They do not stop the boredom
And fill my heart with gloom

The walls that do confine me
Are only in my mind
But I can see right through them
With hope I've come to find

The walls that keep me thankful
That I've a place to rest my head
Hold no place for a false friendship
But the Love of God instead

THE CEDAR TREE

Standing in my backyard
Is majesty in green
Its fern-like boughs that slightly face
The night sky in-between

Tomorrow I may ponder
On life's sweet mystery
But knowing his authority
Is truth enough for me

Because I've been created
From a love that knows no bounds
I thank God for the cedar tree
And its windy, wispy, sounds

There is so much more of this forest green
On earth which can't deceive
So I use my faith and judgement
To show that I believe

And I believe that Jesus died
And he rose again to live
If he had not I'd never know
How love means "I forgive"

Now God answers pray in sweet, uncharted time
Through months, or days, or years between the years
But to know his reason is out of love
God's children know no fears

VICTIM

Many overtures perplex
Sudden seemingly senseless sounds surrounding
solemn
Executed into focused reality
For a bed of forbidden forgotten dreams Of his force
My hatred unannounced
His pressure formidable
His strength unchained
My thoughts strenuous without sounds or interpreta-
tions
Lost in the midst of a sea
Going underground to reach the sky
Not knowing never judging
Innocence unleashing freshness to spoil
Your treatment, the highest of unkind
It never heals

A FLOWER

You and I are a flower
But we live in its bud
Only opening to express love
Gracing the blue skies
In our naked journey
To find a certain peace
And to wake to a gentle rain
We blossom in the spring
And flower all summer long
Deciding to close for colder weather
And freezing over in winter's snow
Picked in the following spring
As we are still together
In the vase we fill
You and I are a flower

INTIMACY

I've found no grounds
For closeness
From spending the night
With a man so much older, a traitor
A child can not find love with a stranger
He steals her innocence
Although she will cry out in fear
And because he really wants her to
A child learns what is taught
And then she becomes older
The impact keeps her in pain hating him
And it haunts her
Reaching out in faith in the
Holy Spirit to guide her
Through her negative experiences
The lust of an evil man
He only wanted me for one night
This is not intimacy, or the love and caring, and respect she
needs and craves
It has not been easy especially for so many years
She never felt worthy or important
And it ricochets in all personal situations when she reaches out
Leaving everyone in the world feeling uncomfortable
Because it always comes back to hurt her like a boomerang
Self-hatred
Cease fire already!
What a crime!
On a little girl!
An uncle having sex with a 7 year old girl!

It makes me sick!
And a 33 year old stranger thinking he has the rights to me
What am I property, because I'm only 12?
What a set-up for more personal abuse
Innocence taken away
Stuck into an adult world
Now old, confused and silent!
Oh pang of tenderness—I shudder, I shudder with guilt and shame
Flashbacks of life filled with pain
Returning again and again
Gaps of missing life blocked out—too painful to endure in consciousness
Mom & Dad where are you?
Oh ya...divorcing
What poetry will bliss my self-hatred
For I cannot love myself
Until God mends me

A STILL LIFE

From my childhood
Discoveries I made of my innocence lost
I shelved my existence he borrowed from time
For a future dance
And with no sun raying through,
My youth vanished like a dying vine in a dark, dense forest
His perfect poisoned kiss, destroyed the wholesome spirit
And truthful mind I once had to offer
Leaving more or less tragic giant cotton-candy memories of childhood
Sweet with the intrigue of innocence...
He forced his mysteriously brilliant pain, while I was undeserving of its shine
Oh evil patron of my shy smile you made me weep my heart out and would not release me...
You made me sing your song...then you played it over and over again
Costing me reality in the pain of your repertoire
So with no more resistance to nightmare dreams I wake once more to a still life....

WHO NEXT?

I shook
I wept
My body numb
The hills echoed shots from guns
And blasts from bombs
Me next?
Who next?
What cruel pain
Do I see before me?
Below the earth
This hollow
Cannot protect forever
Stop the noise
End the strain
Let it rain
Oh God forgive me of my sins
I have no tools to fight
This coming insanity
That will crush my brain
The blistering heat
Turns to coldness in my limbs
I complain to
The skies
Who dies?
Me next?
Who next?

A KISS!

What of a kiss?
The boundaries of our loving limitations lessen,
looking at your assured confidence...
Your eyes tell everything dancing into eternity...
Our souls pressed gently against heartbeats...
Ballerina girl...bold & handsome soul stranger be-
coming
Soul mates of existence here in the connections...
Pleasing vibrations excitedly between our happy
smiles and gentle holding of hands...
Sweet melody of ancient fervours and songs of deliv-
ered sweetness...strong senses of our adjoining
gentle passions...
What of a kiss?
Is it only escaping reality to the solar distances we
cannot find in our galaxy?
Or is it pounding into our bare emotions flesh to
flesh joining in passion?

BE MINE

I ask you to be my Valentine
If you wish with rings and flowers
But all I really care about
Is the time we spend together
The minutes and the hours
I may be asking early
As my heart beats rapid time
Just thinking you'll be here again
For a moment you'll be mine
God doesn't promise that on earth I'll have
Each day filled with pleasure
It's what my heart can do for him
Is the lasting love I treasure
I ask you to be my Valentine
We have known each other a while
I still cannot turn
My head from you
For my Valentine today I want no other

When all hope is gone I write a song...
We'll work it out somehow

When the blues become our truths
And sometimes being close
Makes us not ourselves
But we still love each other
So we'll work it out somehow

You are someone who makes me think
On things that mean so much
And without your touch
I'm lonesome and out of luck
And without your eyes in mine
Where would I be and who do I cry to
You are the angel who believes
I have a place and importance
To hold you and listen
When it's quiet not busy
But it is all a lie

But as we go along
I'm somehow not that strong
My eyes no longer wise
Do not criticize
But I need your peace,
After the war, as we work it out somehow

Think about the storm
   When the rain is pouring down
   My life without you in it
   Is like a heartbeat limit
   The world could never be kind again
If I lost my one and only true love
So I must wait, and remember
What goes around comes around

                    But as we go along
                    I'm not that strong
                    My eyes no longer wise
    Do not criticize But, I need God's peace after the
              war, as we work it out somehow

COMPATIBILITY

I don't know why my heart beats
Ten times faster when you are around
When I'm looking in your eyes
Kissing you, or have an aching in my gut
An almost painful longing
I hope it is not lust
My mind searches for the words
When normally I'm calm
I'm not logical
And my thoughts are silenced
All I'm aware of is me and you
When I'm locked in your gaze
It's heavenly, this attraction
And all in all I've just risked another day
Good peaceful night to you

RAINBOW LIGHTS

Rainbow lights in your eyes
I can see
Clear through to your soul
Beautiful
Petite sun showers and downpours of rain
Those rainbow lights in your eyes
Decide to shine so brightly
That I can see sunshine in your heart
Even if there are grey clouds
I can still see
The shimmer in the rain
The whisper on the wind
The colour throughout
And the rainbow lights in your eyes
Attack my senses
With a breath of vision
A word of peace
A fall scented freshness of you
A touch of harmony
Rainbow lights in your eyes

I'M IN THE MARKET

I'm in the market for Christian friends
Who love the Lord indeed
I'm in the market for Christian friends
So I plant this loving seed

I've felt rejecting loneliness
From those who could care less
I've reached out to those indifferent
Whom I prayed the Lord would bless

But so rewarding is his love at work
I sing a brand new song
It'll tell you that I love the Lord
Because he loved me all along

God blessed me with his mercy
So I'm in this pleasant state
Because I trust the Love of God
That won't go out of date

So with His love so gentle
I hope your heart will hear
The truth God speaks through scripture
And sweet whispers take away all fear

If it's God's love you've accepted
And you choose to do his will
When relationships on earth may fail
His love is sweeter still

I CAN SHARE MY DREAMS

I could share my dreams with you
Then you could share yours too
I pray about it all the time
And hope it would come true

The moon taps on the window sill
And I dream to be with you
I dream of having pillow talks
And feelings things that feel brand new

When our hearts beat wild in harmony
The journey won't seem so long
Having one true love forever
To sing a new love song

Even though we are apart
That circumstance may change
In your absence I grow fonder
As love can rearrange

If I say you're my best friend
And you say that you are mine
We could stay together
As a forever Valentine

I could share my dreams with you
Then you could share yours too
I pray about it all the time
And hope it would come true

I WANT TO BE COOL
LIKE A CALIFORNIAN

I keep water in my fridge
I tried to rollerblade
I made some tie-dyed t-shirts
And I let my blue jeans fade

I want to be cool like a Californian
And have a little fun
I'd like to be a parent
And have a little son

I'd like to be under the Californian sun
By the beach and collect sea shells
I'd like to have a little deck
To smell the sea breeze smells

I'd like to dance at a country dance
On a beach near Hollywood
I'd like my bikini figure back
And work out like I should

But most of all I'd like to have
A Californian smile
And be a star from coast to coast
And be cool for a little while

THE CROWN

We must meet our needs
So we must have God's love
It's a treacherous journey up ahead
That ends up, up above

The King of kings remains as such
We sing the victory song
For it isn't a friend, or sibling, or mum & dad
Who judges right from wrong

The verdict that counts most in life
Is the one that Jesus passes
And if only others think you are honest and good
It's God's judgement of trespasses

If you care enough
About what God has to say
Then you respect him as the Father
And you'll always want to pray

You'll know the death of Jesus proves
You have no better friend
He's just the same yesterday, today, and tomorrow
And he will be till the end

You can fool the world, but not the Heavenly crown
So just ask Jesus to come into your heart
Because he died to protect us from sin and wrong
And were never far apart

TO HOLD YOUR HAND

To hold your hand
Walk a million miles
To hold your hand
Give you all my smiles

To hold your hand
Along the path of life
To hold your hand
Makes everything right

I could close my eyes
Eat a Milky Way
To hold your hand
On a rainy day

The others are crazy
Not the way I am
They say I'm lazy
But I do what I can

Let me cross the wildest river
To get to the other side
To be with you forever
With the Lord who'll be our guide

To hold your hand
Walk in the sand
To hold your hand
Live life as planned

THE WEDDING

Once a feeling
In a while
Love in marriage
Makes me smile

Given friendship
Of a type
Fruitful Love
Becoming ripe

Jesus enters
Into this
Newlyweds
Are filled with bliss

People laughing
Joyful sounds
All together
Love abounds

Toast a cheer
To the past
He has his bride
To love at last

Once a feeling
In a while
Love in marriage
Makes me smile

PROMISES

There are no written promises
For me in most books I've read
It's only in the book of life
Can my heart most freely tred

Nothing holds more certainty
Than the promise of God's love
That floats right down upon us
Like the song of a small dove

Someone I loved had fallen ill
But with this grief, I still saw gain
Without completely destroying my trust in God
It still cause my hear greatest pain

But in my pain, I thanked the Lord
As it drew me near to him
So, instead to drown in sorrow
He gave me strength to swim

Man's promise of man's happiness
May come to being true
But when God gives out a breath of life
I'd take it wouldn't you

The promise that when I die I'll live
Is a sword against all foe
And it is in my love returned to him
That his authority's what I'll know

½ BLUE

I'm ½ blue over you
Only longing here today
That you'll come back to me
And it's forever that you'll stay
I prayed to God to take away the blues
And that you'd be true to me
But you never really loved anyone
And you wanted to be free
I'm ½ blue in love with you
Just missing you so much
I never knew how lonely I'd feel
Or that I'd miss your kiss or touch
God is the sunshine in my day
Against the blueness that I feel
So call me up and pray a while
And tell me you're for real

SONGS FOR YOU

I've been writing songs for you
Because I believe in love
I'm writing songs in the midst of God
He's watching from above

I am not so lost
And I am not so blue
I've never known such joyfulness
And the feeling stays brand new

You'll pat me on my back
With hugs and kisses too
If I'm ever sad or lonely
When I'm very close to you

I feel you in each heartbeat
And you press against my soul
I've never known such passion
I've never reached that goal

I'm sharing a big part of me
I'm sharing it with you
I've learned a lot of many things
Because my life's become brand new

I feel a great undying bond
Between us this is true
God's music is our friend forever
And He'll be there for you

THE DAD OF THE YEAR

10:29 p.m. Barrie, Ontario
Sometimes we don't see eye to eye
And we crowd each other's space
But I don't know what I'd without you
Any time or any place
You may not always understand me
But you do the best you can
What more could a daughter ask for
From this special sort of man
All that I can give you
Are memories from my heart
For the many years I've known you
Together or apart
Sometimes we're both backslidden
But only God knows what's inside
We can pray to him if we make a mistake
And be humbled from our pride
I want to acknowledge you Len, (Pop)
For how much of a friend you are
As a father we can count on
Who's never very far